"L" IS FOR LIBRARY

Sonya Terry

Illustrated by Nicole Wong

Fort Atkinson, Wisconsin

"L" is for Library

By Sonya Terry   Illustrated by Nicole Wong

A is for author,
 painting pictures out of words.

B is for biography,
where true tales of individuals are heard.

C is for the Caldecott,
    awarded for art that pleases the eyes.

D is for the Dewey Decimal System, which helps us organize.

E is for encyclopedia,
  containing volumes of information.

F is for fiction books,
	written from an author's imagination.

G is for guide words,
      that help us find our way.

H is for historical fiction,
great stories about an earlier day.

I is for the illustrator,
who uses pictures to present.

J is for the jacket,
    protecting books from accidents.

K is for a keyword search, that helps us navigate.

L is for the library,
full of books that are really great!

M is for the magazines,
     that arrive each month or week.

N is for nonfiction books,
filled with information that you seek.

O is for overdue,
    when you keep your book too long.

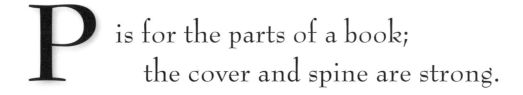

P is for the parts of a book;
the cover and spine are strong.

Q is for quiet,
the best volume for a library voice.

R is for the reference books,
a fact-seeking student's best choice.

S is for shelf markers,
    that help you mark your spot.

T
is for the thesaurus,
which tells you "warm" is another word for "hot."

U is for URL,
a specific Web address.

V is for volunteers,
     a big part of every library's success.

W is for the World Wide Web, full of electronic information.

X is for the Xerox machine, used for document duplication.

Y is for **your** interests,
that change and grow each day.

Z is for catching zzz's—
there's nothing more to say!

Special thanks to God and my family for their support and encouragement.

Special thanks to the dynamic Highsmith team and illustrator Nicole Wong for making this dream possible.

—S.T.

For my mother, for sharing her love of books.

—N.W.